A Curator's Guide
to Exploring Dreams &
Defiance on the Dance Floor

Author: Derrick León Washington, Ph.D.
Illustrator: Olha Aleksandrova

Copyright ©2025 Derrick León Washington

All rights reserved. No part of this publication may be reproduced, distributed, or transmitted in any form or by any means, including photocopying, recording, or other electronic or mechanical methods, without the prior written permission of the publisher, except in the case of brief quotations in critical articles, reviews, and workshops. Teachers are welcome to use the story for class; please give **Urban Stomp** credit.

Written by Derrick León Washington, Ph.D.
Illustrations by Olha Aleksandrova
Cover Design by Derrick León Washington, Ph.D.

Published by the Urban Stomp Project in 2025

For more information visit:
https://www.mcny.org/exhibition/urban-stomp and www.urbanstomp.org

Printed in the USA

Library of Congress Control Number: 2025906847
Softcover ISBN: 979-8-218-99608-6
Hardcover ISBN: 979-8-89901-070-5
Electronic Book ISBN: 979-8-89901-071-2

From the Author

Urban Stomp is a vibrant celebration of social dance cultures, where every step forms a powerful connection to shared traditions and creativity. The journey begins with dance, but it doesn't end there—it extends to food, music, fashion, the spaces where dance happens, and the conversations long after the dance has ended. These aspects of dance cultures shape every step and every moment.

The exhibition at the Museum of the City of New York marks several firsts in the realm of museum experiences. Primarily, it's the first exhibition to center interconnected social dance cultures. Beyond simply highlighting these cultures, it is the first to connect 19th century dance styles to 20th and 21st century dance cultures. It integrates actual dance practice in the galleries, featuring over 20 social dance tutorial films and 11 dance floor immersive installation films. Building upon a previous exhibition I curated, *Rhythm & Power: Salsa* in New York, this is also the first museum exhibition to open up a conversation about four distinct styles of Salsa dancing, demonstrating how they have shaped dance floors, both locally and globally. Likewise, it's the first to center social dance practices in styles where music and dance are inseparable, including Cumbia, Merengue, Contra, Cumbia Sonidera, Bhangra, Dabka, and Bachata. Additionally, it's the first to showcase the hip-hop dance styles of Litefeet and Sturdy—dances which, although now going viral on social media, originally grew from a continuum of hip-hop styles birthed in New York City.

This book presents my perspective, offering an experiential journey that explores the themes of the exhibition it complements. As you engage with the exhibition, or with social dance through this book, I encourage you to write notes in the margins, reflect on the "Call to Action" prompts, play music, and, by all means, dance—alone or with others. At the exhibition and its related programs, share your discoveries and social dance experiences with others.

See you on the dance floor!

> Derrick León Washington
> Curator, *Urban Stomp: Dreams & Defiance on the Dance Floor*

Urban Stomp Legacy Note: I launched the first iteration of the larger Urban Stomp project in 2018 to explore the connections among live music, social dance, food cultures, and neighborhoods in New York City, with a focus on the relationships between Black, Caribbean, Latino, and Jewish communities. Working with community-based organizations like the Clemente Soto Vélez Cultural & Educational Center, and institutions like New York University, the project featured an extensive, interactive program series across NYC neighborhoods—including a short documentary film. This work laid the foundation for an evening-length lecture-performance at Lincoln Center for the Performing Arts in 2019.

In 2022, the project expanded with a documentary collaboration at the iconic Apollo Theater and a teaching artist training series at Rutgers University. The relationships formed with individuals, communities, and institutions laid the foundation for securing objects that would ultimately shape the Urban Stomp exhibition in 2025. The exhibition and program series at the Museum of the City of New York (April 11, 2025– February 22, 2026) continues the goals of:

- Creating spaces of multidisciplinary learning, fun, and collective joy;
- Cultivating sustainable relationships with artists, communities, and those who advocate for human rights; and
- Expanding curatorial practice and impact by centering interactivity.

Contents

Introduction 1

CHAPTER 1
YOU ARE INVITED: BALLS, BALLROOMS & BARS 5
    The Foxtrot 9
    Castle Walk 10
    Animal Dances 12
    Call to Action 14
        You Are Invited to Balls, Ballrooms, Bars, and Where We're Safe 14

    Dance & Movement Practice 16
        Dance Starts with Movement 16

    Object Highlights in the Exhibition Section 17

CHAPTER 2
IT DON'T MEAN A THING (IF IT AIN'T GOT THAT SWING) 18
    Rooted Jazz Dances 20
    Lindy Hop 22
    Call to Action 24
        Create Spaces that Feel like Home 24

    Dance & Movement Practice 26
        Start Your Day with a Strut 26

    Object Highlights in the Exhibition Section 28

CHAPTER 3
¡WEPA! FREEDOM DREAMS FROM MAMBO TO MERENGUE 30
    Salsa Dance Styles 32
    Salsa Caleña and Rueda de Casino 34
    Bachata Beats and Merengue Moves 36
    Call to Action 38
        All Styles Are Celebrated Here 38

    Dance & Movement Practice 40
        Dancing in the Home or Going Outside 40

    Object Highlights in the Exhibition Section 42

CHAPTER 4
THE CYPHER: BREAKS & BREAKING BARRIERS 45

- Hip-Hop Dances. 46
- Hustle 48
- Vogue 51
- Call to Action 52
    - *A Cypher to Keep the Negativity Out and Positivity In* 52
- Dance & Movement Practice 54
    - *The Warm-Up*. 54
- Object Highlights in the Exhibition Section 55

CHAPTER 5
ARE WE ALL CITY YET? TRADITIONS REMIXED. 56

- Bhangra 58
- Dabka. 60
- Contra 62
- Yiddish Dance 64
- Cumbia and Cumbia Sonidera 66
- Chinatown Block Party Bounce 68
- Native American Dances and the Powwow 70
- Dance & Movement Practice 73
    - *Start Somewhere - Let's Try Bhangra*. 73
- Call to Action 74
    - *See You Outside* 74
- Object Highlights in the Exhibition Section 76

Conclusion. 78
Urban Stomp Dance Tutorials Checklist 80
All Dancing Allowed! Checklist. 82
Exhibition Scavenger Hunt. 83
Places to Learn, Practice & Social Dance 87
Object Highlights in the Exhibition by Section 90
About the Author. 97
About the Illustrator. 100
Exhibition Dance Video Tutorial Film Credits 101
Exhibition Immersive Dance Floor Film Credits. 103
Bibliography 105

Introduction

Urban Stomp is a metaphor for building community through the power of social dance. It celebrates legacies, life, humility, and a defiant joy that resonates both on and off the dance floor. As the first exhibition of its kind at a museum or institution, it explores over 200 years of social dance in New York City, from the ballrooms and bars of the 19th century to the parks, living rooms, and clubs of today. The exhibition illuminates how New York's dance cultures and their related dance floors create spaces of collective celebration and social possibilities that have an impact everywhere.

I created this book as a companion to the *Urban Stomp: Dreams & Defiance on the Dance Floor* exhibition and program series (2025 – 2026) at the Museum of the City of New York. Inside, you'll find my suggestions for engaging with the exhibition, from dance warm-up exercises and exhibition highlights to a trivia scavenger hunt and recommendations for social dance events across New York City you can attend. Along the way, you'll encounter prompts meant to inspire reflection, encourage you to dance, explore the broader communities connected to the social dances, and appreciate some of the variations within each dance style.

"Urban" in the title represents the vibrant metropolis that is New York City—a complex melting pot of cultures, ideas, and people with roots from all over the world. It's a city where diversity ignites creative collaborations that are the soul of the social dances shared in this book.

"Stomp" is the heartbeat—the rhythms that tie music and dance together. It's the percussive pulse found in swing and Afro-Latin music. Musicians *stomp* the ground to keep musical time. The stomps are the swingouts in Lindy Hop and the *shines*—improvisational solo steps—in Salsa dancing. It's the *dip* in Vogue and the literal stomps in Bhangra dancing. These stomps are connected through shared histories, or mixing, contributing to the vibrant energy of the city.

Urban Stomp, as a theory, is a call to action—a way to curate exhibitions, or spaces, which encourages community collaboration to have a greater impact. By including community in the curatorial process, the exhibition drew together over 300 objects, as well as over 90 dancers who traveled to the Museum and central Brooklyn to create dance films for the exhibit's various sections.

Urban Stomp, as a teaching philosophy, values diverse ways of learning. This is the reason visitors are invited to dance in the galleries of the exhibition. It's the reason this companion book encourages readers to dance, even daily; understanding this is an avenue for personal and social inspiration.

The book's chapters reflect the exhibition's section titles. Chapter 1, *You Are Invited: Balls, Ballrooms & Bars*, explores how social dance became one of the most important forms of entertainment in New York City in the mid-19th century through the 1910s, providing a way to meet potential partners, project social status, and celebrate shared cultures. Chapter 2, *It Don't Mean a Thing (If It Ain't Got That Swing)*, discusses how dances rooted in jazz music offer new possibilities for collective celebration and social relationships. Chapter 3, *¡Wepa! Freedom Dreams from Mambo to Merengue*, examines how dancers hold, give, and share space through social dance cultures with roots in the Caribbean. Chapter 4, *The Cypher: Breaks & Breaking Barriers*, looks at how the dances of Hip-Hop, Hustle, and Vogue help people create chosen families and alternative spaces for artistic freedom. Chapter 5, *Are We All City Yet? Traditions Remixed*, illuminates how NYC dancers engage with traditions, often reworking social dances by 'remixing' them aesthetically or practicing them in new geographic or social contexts.

While this book, like the exhibition, roughly moves chronologically from the early 1800s to the present, it presents these dance cultures—though they may have originated decades ago—as dynamic, with no fixed end date. To demonstrate equity among social dances, all social dances are capitalized.

Each hand-drawn illustration commissioned for this book, provides a glimpse into the cultures that have shaped these dances, past and present. The living rooms, cookouts, block parties, festivals, clubs, dance studios—anywhere people gather to social dance—serve as the backdrop for the illustrations. The illustrations offer a glimpse into the context of each dance, allowing the view to immerse themselves more fully. The drawings are inspired by the author's experiences as a lifelong dancer and 20+ years of anthropological research.

Below are some prompts to guide your exploration of the illustrations:

- **What do you see?** Take a moment to look at the scene. What's happening in the picture?
- **Who is in the picture?** Notice the people in the image. What are they doing? Dancing, talking, or is it something else?
- **Where is this happening?** Is it at a club, on the street, or in a living room? Notice how the space is connected to the dance style.

- **How do the people feel?** Look at their faces and body language. Are they smiling, serious, focused, defiant, or any another emotion?

- **What do the illustrations say about culture?** Think about the dance moves, the clothing, or the decorations in the background. How does it reflect some of the traditions and values of that community?

- **How does it make you feel?** Does the picture inspire excitement, curiosity, or a desire to learn more? What emotions or memories does it bring up for you?

YOU ARE INVITED: BALLS, BALLROOMS & BARS

The first dances that centered around community, in what is now New York City, were performed by the Lenape people, who called this land Lenapehoking. When the Dutch arrived and renamed the area New Amsterdam (1624), followed by the English who then renamed it New York (1664), the city's identity shifted and continued to change over time. Despite these shifts, social dance continued to play a significant role in the lives of the people in this ever-expanding city. Dance floors weren't merely about the steps; they were the stage where the city's diverse people gathered, mingled, strengthened relationships, or even projected power.

In a city as vast as New York, the dance scenes were far from uniform. The elite sought out exclusive, private balls, while the middle class filled rented halls for organized social events. Meanwhile, the working class found their rhythm in local bars, churches, and community halls. Whether it was at a lively gathering or an elegant ball, social dancing offered a moment to showcase status, to embrace culture, or to find common ground with others.

By the late 1890s, the city was humming with new, soulful energy. Over the next decades, African American migrants from the South and Midwest brought with them new rhythms and bold dances from bars and "jook joints," igniting a movement that would transform New York City's soundscape. Ragtime quickly became the popular music of the day, fueling a revolution in social dance and music that was unlike anything that had come before.

For many, these dances marked a profound change from the past. They complemented the driving, rapid rhythms of ragtime piano playing. The city became emboldened by this vibrant sound and style that would slowly reshape the dance world for years to come, as rhythm, improvisation, and artistic freedom took center stage.

This book is dedicated to the elders and youth who remind us to dance defiantly and joyously every single day.

Your spirit inspires us to keep moving forward, no matter what life brings.

Published on the occasion of the presentation of the exhibition, this book is also dedicated to the staff at the Museum of the City of New York, with a special thanks to Sarah Henry, whose collaboration as a curator and advocate helped make the exhibition at the Museum a reality.

The Foxtrot

The Foxtrot wasn't just a dance; it was a snapshot of a time full of social change and excitement. In the 1910s, the world was shifting, and the Foxtrot became a way to express a cool sophistication, exemplified by the ragtime rhythms made popular in the San Juan Hill and Harlem neighborhoods of Manhattan.

With its smooth walking steps, mixed with sharp accents, the Foxtrot expressed the popular rhythms of the day. In the taverns and bars that "respectable" folk often avoided, people from different ethnic backgrounds would come together, crossing social lines to celebrate the syncopated music and its accompanying dances. The dance floor became a place where elegance met energy, where tradition met new social possibilities.

Castle Walk

Starting in the 1910s, the Castle Walk infused lively energy into the dance floor. Imagine dancers gliding around with smooth, effortless moves, adding a little side-to-side shuffle, a sway of the hips, and a touch of grace. The "Walk" was about embracing the rhythm of the music as though you were casually strolling through a grand ballroom without a care in the world. It was all about showing off poise and musicality—-perfect for the Jazz Age's love of revelry with style. With its fluid motion and relaxed aesthetics, the Castle Walk offered a refreshing contrast to dances like the Waltz, which required a stiffer, more rigid body frame.

The dance was created by Vernon and Irene Castle. The Castles played a pivotal role in bringing ragtime dances into the public eye. This famous couple helped popularize dances like the tango, foxtrot, and one-step, while distancing themselves from what they referred to as the 'hideous gyrations' and 'salaciousness' of the African American, Afro-Latino, and folk dances that inspired them. While they helped bring these dances into mainstream popularity, it is important to recognize and respect the cultural roots and contributions of the communities from which they originated.

Animal Dances

Bars, taverns, and speakeasies became the spaces where a raucous variation of One-Step and Two-Step dances proliferated. People in the 1910s curled their fingers and flexed their arms to dance like grizzly bears—yes, people did this—and danced like bunny rabbits, turkeys, and other assorted animals during the 1900s and through to the 1920s.

Dances like the Turkey Trot, the Bunny Hug, and the Grizzly Bear took over the dance floors and complemented the ragtime music that played throughout New York City at that time. Originating in African American communities, these dances blended elements of African rhythms and movement styles with ragtime and jazz music. They were a celebration of self-expression and the power of music to move the body in new, uninhibited ways. As these exhilarating rhythms fueled the dance floors, it wasn't just the steps that were new but the very spirit of the time: bold and ready to break through the social boundaries that marginalized whole groups of people.

Teaching the Cubs how to Grizzly Bear

Call to Action
You Are Invited to Balls, Ballrooms, Bars, and Where We're Safe

The first call to action is to just dance! You don't need a fancy ballroom or an invitation to an exclusive ball to get yourself moving. Although musicians like Scott Joplin, and big bands, like James Reese Europe's Clef Club Orchestra are no longer around to perform ragtime music on a daily basis, it doesn't stop us from celebrating their music through dance. A central goal of *Urban Stomp* is to create a space where *everyone* can take part, feel safe, and feel valued. After all, most of the dances in this section originated as community dance cultures where people expressed new possibilities for celebration.

Whether you "lead" or "follow" in couple or group dances, your dance contributes to a conversation with others—a dancing story that couldn't happen without *you*.

Invited to Come As You Are

Dance & Movement Practice
Dance Starts with Movement

Walking is the foundation for the dances featured in this section of the book as well as the exhibition. Whether alone, as a couple, or in a group, why not try these walking exercises to start your One-Step, Two-Step, Foxtrot, Castle Walk, or any other social dance journey.

- Walk clockwise in a circle (maintain a circle as you follow the next set of instructions)
- Walk backward
- Walk forward
- Walk in slow motion
- Walk forward at medium speed
- Walk fast like you're late for school or work
- Walk forward at medium speed
- Walk 'slow-slow, quick-quick'
- Walk forward at medium speed
- Walk like a Turkey, Grizzly Bear, Rabbit, or Kangaroo (your choice of animal dance)
- Walk forward at medium speed
- Walk arm-in-arm with another person, if someone's there with you
- Lead the person
- Switch and be led by that person
- Walk forward at medium speed
- Walk synchronized with everyone else
- Walk to the beat of the music if available
- End

Feel free to write down how that felt. You can include your own steps, too. Will you try the Waltz, Two-Step, Foxtrot, Castle Walk, or Animal Dances? Look at a few options to learn in the *Places to Learn, Practice & Social Dance* section of this book.

Object Highlights in the Exhibition Section

Invitation, Ticket, and Dance Card for the Prince of Wales Ball
October 12, 1860
MCNY, Gift of Mrs. Stowe Phelps, 1961

"Order of Dancing at the Wedding of Mrs. Wells"
1865
Wood, white silk satin, white silk fringe, and gilt metallic trim
MCNY, Bequest of Miss Caroline Thorn Wells, 1950

Ball Gown
House of Worth, design house, designed by Charles Frederick Worth
1860
Silver and silk compound weave with peach ciselé velvet in floral and foliate motifs, white silk satin, and white silk lace
MCNY, Gift of Miss Sarah Gardiner, 1939

Fan
1850–60
Paper, mother-of-pearl, ink, paint, and silver-tone metal
MCNY, Bequest of Miss Katherine Van Wyck Haddock, 1951

Dance Shoes Worn by Irene Castle
Martin & Martin
ca. 1914
Orange and black silk satin and leather
MCNY, Gift of Mrs. Irene Castle, 1947

Hair Belonging to Irene Castle
Irene Castle
1914
Human hair
MCNY, Gift of Mrs. George Enzinger, 1948

Cylinder Phonograph
Edison Home Model A
The Edison Speaking Phonograph Company
1903
Metal and wood
MCNY, Gift of Rebecca, Amiel, and Juliet Weisfogel, 2025

IT DON'T MEAN A THING (IF IT AIN'T GOT THAT SWING)

In the years between the World Wars (1918 – 1939), New York City swayed to a new rhythmic revolution in music and dance. The 1920s, or the "Jazz Age," was powered by the Charleston, its carefree steps sweeping through speakeasies and nightclubs.

Then, as the music evolved, swing music arrived; a pulsating jazz style that laid the foundation for different jazz dances, including the Lindy Hop. At places like Harlem's Savoy Ballroom, dancers of all abilities glided, swiveled, and bounced to some of the best Jazz musicians to ever pick up an instrument.

In the 1930s, swing music wasn't just a sound; it was a feeling that shaped a vision of what the U.S. would strive to become—a country where people from all backgrounds could come together to create beautiful music and share space on and off the dance floor. Swing and Lindy Hop continue to bring people together nearly a century after their creation.

Rooted Jazz Dances

Jazz dances include pulses, walks, vibrations, and taps that are in dynamic conversation with the music. Rooted Jazz dances are the foundational styles of jazz dance that emerged in African American communities in the early 1900s. These dances are "rooted" in the cultural and historical context of various time periods. They thrived on the streets, at house parties, or "cutting contests" that happened outside of concert halls.

Spreading outside the African American communities, the dances continued to evolve as various people and groups adopted them. Some significant Rooted Jazz dancers include: Josephine Baker, George "Shorty" Snowden, Norma Miller, The Nicholas Brothers, Dean Collins, Mama Lou Parks, Pepsi Bethel, Katherine Dunham, Al Minns, and Leon James.

Lindy Hop

Lindy Hop emerged in Harlem in the late 1920s as an amalgamation of different dances, with George "Shorty" Snowden and Mattie Purnell shaping its early form. It was the collective energy and creativity of Harlem and New York City dancers that added and innovated countless moves, making it a dance born from the people.

The dance is the physical embodiment of swing music. Dancers interpret music with subtle pulses or a smooth elastic movement that includes frequent moments of creative improvisation.

Call to Action
Create Spaces that Feel like Home

Urban Stomp is not just about dance steps; it's also a method for creating spaces for social dance, music, and community. From the "Home of the Happy Feet"—a nickname for the Savoy Ballroom in Harlem—to the Kelly Street Block Festivals in the Bronx, social dance plays a vital role in so many social gatherings.

You too can create your own social dance space!

It's important to create a space where everyone feels comfortable and free to dance or simply to look on from the sidelines. Start by clearing the floor of anything that could cause someone to trip. Make room for people to rest with comfortable seating. Home-cooked food and drinks help to create a more relaxed, communal atmosphere. Small touches, like plants, soft lighting, and even a wooden floor, can make the space feel inviting.

Some people might feel okay being recorded for social media, while others might prefer not to be—it's good practice to ask before posting on social media so that everyone feels like they can dance without the need to perform for the world.

Different social music and dance styles bring their own unique energy and vibe, so create accordingly. Whether the music is fast and upbeat or slow and smooth, creating an environment where everyone feels safe and welcomed is at the core of *Urban Stomp*.

Dance & Movement Practice
Start Your Day with a Strut

Lindy Hop jazz dances include pulses, walks, vibrations, skips, and taps that engage in a dynamic conversation with the music. Jazz dancing has a way of making the day, well, brighter! What better way to start your day than with a dance?

Before checking emails or scrolling through social media in the morning, try dancing the Charleston variations, Tacky Annie, Boogie Forward/Back, Fishtails, or the Shim-Sham. Luckily, most of these dances are in the dance tutorials or in the dance floor films in the exhibition. There are dozens of other dances you could do though. What's most important is to do what feels good for your body.

Rooted Jazz dances are inseparable from the music that inspired them. Below are some iconic songs to dance to. All these artists have some of their original instruments displayed in the exhibition.

Benny Goodman:
"Stompin' at the Savoy" (1936)
"One O'Clock Jump" (1937)
"Why Don't You Do Right?" (1942)

Lester Young
"Oh, Lady Be Good" (1936)
"Honeysuckle Rose" (1937)

Cootie Williams
"Somebody's Gotta Go" (1944)
"Fly Right" (1944)

Miles Davis
"All Blues" (1959)

"When Lights Are Low" (1944)
"Mystery" (1959)
"Freedom Jazz Dance" (1966)

Billie Holiday
"Them There Eyes" (1939)
"Billie's Blues" (1941)
"Swing, Brother, Swing" (1939)

Object Highlights in the Exhibition Section

Josephine Baker Dancing the Charleston
Stanislaw Julian Ignacy Ostoróg, known as Walery
1926
Reproduction
National Portrait Gallery, Smithsonian Institution

Louis Armstrong's Trumpet
Selmer
1933
Steel and brass
Courtesy of Institute of the Louis Armstrong House Museum

Pages from Louis Armstrong's Manuscript Autobiography
1925
Courtesy of Institute of Jazz Studies, Rutgers University-Newark, Institute of Jazz Studies artifact collection

Untitled (Duke Ellington with Floating Piano)
Ed Dwight
ca. 1980
Bronze
Art & Artifacts Division, Schomburg Center for Research in Black Culture, The New York Public Library, Astor, Lenox and Tilden Foundations

The Frankie Manning Quilt
Jen Pringle
2009, tee-shirts from 1985 – 2009
Cotton quilt made of commemorative tee-shirts
Collection of Lana Turner, New York

Handbill, Savoy Ballroom
March 21, 1937
Courtesy of the International Lindy Hop Championships Museum

Benny Goodman's Clarinet
Buffet-Crampon
ca. 1960
Grenadilla, nickel-silver, plastic, and other materials
Lent by The Metropolitan Museum of Art, Gift of William F. Hyland, in memory of Theodore and Margaret Hyland, his parents, 1998

Lester Young's New Wonder 1 Tenor Saxophone
C. G. Conn
1914
Gold-plated brass
Courtesy of Institute of Jazz Studies, Rutgers University-Newark, Institute of Jazz Studies artifact collection

Cootie Williams's Long-Model Cornet
C. G. Conn
1968
Brass
Courtesy of Institute of Jazz Studies, Rutgers University-Newark, Institute of Jazz Studies artifact collection

Miles Davis's Trumpet
Martin
1964
Brass
Courtesy of Institute of Jazz Studies, Rutgers University-Newark, Institute of Jazz Studies artifact collection

Jack Teagarden's Trombone
C.G. Conn, mouthpiece made by Vincent Bach Corp.
ca. 1925
Brass, copper, and zinc alloy
Courtesy of Institute of Jazz Studies, Rutgers University-Newark, Institute of Jazz Studies artifact collection

Bracelets Worn by Billie Holiday
Metal and rhinestones
20th century
Courtesy of Institute of Jazz Studies, Rutgers University-Newark, Institute of Jazz Studies artifact collection

¡WEPA! FREEDOM DREAMS FROM MAMBO TO MERENGUE

"¡Wepa!"—an exclamation from the Caribbean—expresses the spirit of social dances that are about play, connection, and rhythm. It's a call, a greeting, and an affirmation.

Afro-Latin rhythms and dance styles reshaped New York City's social dance scene, leaving their mark on everything from the Tango in the 1910s, to Mambo's rise in the 1950s, to Salsa, which became a powerful cultural movement in the late 1960s. By the 1980s, the soulful steps of Merengue and Bachata—rooted in Dominican culture—started to dominate the city's dance floors. In the mid-2020s, DJs play dembow, reggaeton, and Latin trap on the same dance floors as Salsa. Dancers might even incorporate a Bachata step before transitioning into dancing Perreo.

These dances reflect a broader, inclusive vision of what it means to be "American"—a blend of cultures, people, and rhythms from throughout the Americas.

Salsa Dance Styles

There are many ways to interpret salsa music. One popular style, often called "New York style salsa," changes direction on the second and sixth beat of the musical bar. This form, also known as Salsa On2, closely follows the rhythmic styling of New York salsa music.

There's also Salsa On3, a style that accents the third beat of the musical bar. This style is commonly danced at family gatherings, cultural festivals, and annual community concerts in East Harlem, South Williamsburg, Bushwick, the Lower East Side, and Orchard Beach (in the Bronx).

Rather than focusing on fixed timing, other dancers follow the rhythm of the music and the movements of their partners.

Salsa Caleña and Rueda de Casino

Another style danced, primarily in Queens, is the *Salsa Caleña*, a dance originally from Cali, Colombia, characterized by rapid footwork and knees lifted up high. A dance born in what's commonly referred to as the 'capital of Salsa' (Cali), it blends all the best elements that Salsa dancing has to offer. It has been reinvigorated in Queens, New York, where it's been influenced by other styles of Salsa and social dance.

Rueda de Casino predates Salsa dancing and is danced in a circle, usually with three or more couples, who change partners moving counterclockwise. *Casino* (commonly called "Cuban Salsa" in the U.S.) has developed a New York City flair by incorporating partner turns and solo styling (called "shines") from Salsa On2.

Bachata Beats and Merengue Moves

As the Dominican New York community surged in the 1980s—eventually becoming New York City's largest Latino ethnic group—they helped popularize two distinct dance forms that transformed the New York social dance scene.

Bachata Urbana, as a music and dance style, arose in the 1990s in Washington Heights and the Bronx, within miles of the birthplace of hip-hop, blending hip-hop and R&B with traditional Bachata sounds and dance moves from the Dominican Republic.

In parallel, the high-energy music of *Merengue Típico* provides the soundtrack for a dance of the same name that has a devoted multi-generational following of New Yorkers.

Even though Bachata and Merengue are often danced at the same gatherings, they bring different energies to New York City's dance floors. Bachata, danced at studios as well as informal gatherings, is arguably the most popular social dance of the mid-2020s.

Call to Action
All Styles Are Celebrated Here

There are never-ending debates on what's the "best" style of Salsa dancing, or what style of Latin/Afro-Latin social dance is the most authentic. With *Urban Stomp,* all social dance styles are welcome!

Each style honors those who came before us. The sounds of hip-hop, reggaeton, soca, salsa, bachata, and merengue típico fill the air during the summer months in New York City. There is no competition, just complete respect for their diverse roots and routes that span the globe.

This call to action is simple but impactful. Try dancing to salsa songs that you're not as familiar with. Experiment with a Salsa dance style or timing that challenges you. Pay attention to how this style interprets the music. In addition to Salsa, try dancing Bachata and Merengue in spaces you're not accustomed to. Notice the variety of styles that flourish in New York City. Most importantly, let these social dances remind you of the power in giving, holding, and sharing space with others.

Dance & Movement Practice
Dancing in the Home or Going Outside

What styles of Salsa, Bachata, or Merengue will you try? Do you prefer open position (a dance hold where partners are in close physical contact) or closed opposition (where partners are connected by both hands with outstretched arms)? Do you prefer fast or slow music? Where do you like, or would like, to dance?

One of the best ways to learn social dance is to explore. Below are links to classes, socials, and festivals in New York City.

Salsa
- **Salsa On2**
  - Eddie and Maria Torres
    https://www.eddietorresny.com
  - Karel Flores
    https://www.instagram.com/karelflores/?hl=en
  - Piel Canela Dance School
    https://pielcaneladancers.com
  - Frankie Martinez
    https://www.frankiemartinez.org/nyc-classes
  - Latin Mondays at Taj hosted by Talia Castro-Pozo and classes with Marlon International
- **Salsa Caleña**
  - Cali Salsa Pal Mundo
    https://www.instagram.com/calisalsanyc/?hl=en

- **Cuban Salsa**
  - Fuakata-Cuban Salsa NY
    https://www.instagram.com/fuakata_salsa_nyc/?hl=en

- **Salsa Dance in the Home / Salsa On3**
  - La Sala de Pepe
    https://www.lasaladepepe.org
  - Mama Juanas (Bronx), Salsa Tuesdays
    https://www.instagram.com/mamajuanabronx/?hl=en
  - 116th Street Festival
    https://116thstfestival.com
  - Orchard Beach Salsa Sundays
    Usually from noon until 5pm or 6pm, Plaza-Bandshell in Section 9 at Orchard Beach
  - 111th Street Old-Timers Day
    http://www.streetplay.com/events/111street2000.htm

Bachata
- Areíto Arts
  https://www.areitoarts.com
- ¡Dame Tu Pasito!
  https://www.instagram.com/dame.tu.pasito

Merengue
- Piel Canela Dance School
  https://pielcaneladancers.com

Object Highlights in the Exhibition Section

Dress owned by Celia Cruz

20th century
Quilted polyester
Courtesy of Celia Cruz Legacy Project

Shoes Owned by Celia Cruz

Miguel Nieto
20th century
Leather, rhinestones, satin, aluminum, vinyl, and rubber
Courtesy of Celia Cruz Legacy Project

Red Shirt, Pants, and Shoes Worn by Eddie Torres

Shoes by Alvarez Dance Shoes, shirt by Maria Torres, and pants by unknown maker
ca. 2017 – 2022
Shoes: leather; shirt: silk; and pants: polyester
Courtesy of Eddie Torres, Mambo King

Tito Puente's Timbales

Latin Percussion, Inc.
20th century
Steel, plastic, and ink with chrome plating
Courtesy of Tito Puente Jr.

Fania All-Stars Jacket Owned by Rubén Blades

ca. 1977
Wool and leather
Courtesy of Rubén Blades

Poster, "1er Festival del Merengue!"

1977
CUNY
Dominican Studies Institute Special Collections

Güira and Gancho
Blanco Custom
2019
Metal and wood
Courtesy of Areíto Arts

Aventura at an Awards Ceremony
2000s
Inkjet print
Courtesy of Juan and Judy Santos

THE CYPHER: BREAKS & BREAKING BARRIERS

In the 1960s and 1970s, New York City's dance scene exploded with boundary-pushing styles where dancers and audiences formed shared creative spaces. Hip-hop dances, Hustle, and Vogue may look worlds apart, but they all have one thing in common—they emerged in a five-mile stretch between Harlem and the South Bronx.

At the heart of these styles is the concept of being seen. In Hip-hop, the "Cypher," or Circle, creates a space where dancers can challenge each other in a battle or exchange movement ideas in noncompetitive ways. The Hustle uses partner-switching in Circles to showcase skilled dancers' mastery of the style. In Vogue, the community might use a Circle or open it up to create a Runway, enhancing the social performance. Whether it's a Cypher, Circle, or Runway, these spaces become opportunities for people to share their personal and collective stories on the dance floor.

Style with Ease

Hip-Hop Dances

Hip-hop dances are a manifestation of the broader and constantly evolving cultures of hip-hop. Beginning in African American, Black, and Caribbean street cultures in various parts of the United States, they're now a global social dance form, fueled by adaptation and innovation.

Breaking exemplifies how New Yorkers share and physically take space when none is made available to them. While you might not be able to enter every Cypher, if you're new to the dance, it's a space where people can give honest feedback on your skills and ways in which you can grow.

In the 1980s and 1990s, dancers blended elements of Breaking with other Hip-hop styles, House, Funk, and Rooted Jazz dances. Moves like "The Running Man," "The Wop," and "Roger Rabbit" were created or reimagined, drawing inspiration from past dance forms while adding a new twist.

Saturday Stoop Sessions with the Epic Edges Gurlz & Astros Krew

Hustle

Known as Hustle, New York Hustle, or Latin Hustle, these names all refer to a partnered dance that became a staple of R&B, soul, and disco music in the 1970s. Born in the South Bronx, it was a creation by New Yorkers, particularly those of Puerto Rican descent, who were living in neighborhoods facing the challenges of deindustrialization, disinvestment, and civil unrest.

What began as a freeform dance with teens grooving to music without rigid guidelines quickly spread across the city and beyond, reaching global popularity. Thanks to the film *Saturday Night Fever*, the Hustle became a cultural phenomenon. Beyond this film, New Yorkers continued to celebrate the Hustle, a dance that transcended both social borders and generations.

The Paradise Garage in Soho was famous as an incubator of the vibrant club cultures of the 1970s and 1980s. Known as a place where people of all identities and backgrounds came together, it re-shaped many dances, including the Hustle. At the Garage, the Hustle became a symbol of self-expression, blending both partnered and solo dance elements.

Some might incorrectly call the Hustle a 1970s trend, but much like Lindy Hop and Palladium Mambo before it, it reflects the idea of 'democracy on the dance floor,' where everyone can participate and express themselves freely.

Vogue

Voguing, a form of dance that includes stylized posing partially inspired by fashion models on the runway, martial arts, and the covers of *Vogue* magazine, has roots in New York City's African American and Latino LGBTQIA+ houses of the late 1960s and 1970s.

The "houses," which function like extended families who provide support and community for members, are the incubator of the dance. Whether dancing Old Way, New Way, or Vogue Femme Dramatics, Vogue shows how dance is an avenue for people to create chosen families.

Forms of Vogue

Old Way or Pop, Dip, and Spin (Created Pre-1990s)
This form focuses on lines, form, and improvisational wit, choosing distinct poses inspired by fashion magazines, pantomime, Egyptian figure illustrations, Breaking, the military and Kung Fu imagery.

New Way
This uses more fluid and rapid moves, incorporating ways to take to the floor with a "Catwalk" or "Duckwalk," as well as exaggerated body movements, often involving contortion, or "Clicking."

Vogue Femme Soft
This form celebrates femininity and flamboyance with wild, often risqué gestures and body language. The elements of Vogue—spins and dips, catwalk, duckwalk, hand performance, and floor performance—in this style of Voguing are all fluid and help to tell a story.

Vogue Femme Dramatics
This style incorporates acrobatics and complex stunts into the performance, including spins, flips and, most notably, dips—this being one of the most emblematic moves of modern Vogue.

Hunt the House Down!

Call to Action
A Cypher to Keep the Negativity Out and Positivity In

The concept of the Cypher, originating in continental Africa and reimagined in the Americas, serves as a powerful space where people come together to share dance steps, energy, and personal stories. Another example of this concept is the "Soul Train Line," where people form two lines and take turns dancing down the middle, showcasing individual expression while others maintain the rhythm.

The Catwalk, rooted in parade traditions, is a prominent feature at Vogue balls where the boundary between audience and performers blurs, creating an immersive experience that celebrates both individuality and community.

The Cypher, the Soul Train Line, and the Catwalk are ways to witness and be witnessed in dance. Try one of these social dance practices to help your dance become more social and inviting. Lowering the barrier for participation makes it easier for everyone to join in. In this way, ultimately, the main goal of *Urban Stomp* is to create moments of community, freedom, and connection.

Walk it Out

Dance & Movement Practice
The Warm-Up

Life and work can be hectic, but playing your favorite Hip-Hop, Ballroom, House, or Disco music can have a wonderful effect on your mood. And if there's music, there can be dance! Whether it's to start your day, before a big work/school presentation, or after a long workday—dance it out!

Get the Body Moving (2 minutes)
- Bounce lightly on your feet with your knees slightly bent
- Let your arms sway naturally with the beat
- Focus on feeling the music and getting your body moving to the rhythm

Neck and Shoulders (2 minutes)
- Drop your head to one side and roll it in a full circle
- Switch directions and roll your shoulders forward in big circles
- Then roll your shoulders backward in big circles

Arm Swings & Chest Pops (3 minutes)
- Stand with your feet a hip's width apart and swing your arms forward and back in big circles
- Pop your chest forward and back in rhythm whilst letting your arms swing
- Keep the upper body loose and relaxed

Leg Swings & Knee Bends (3 minutes)
- Swing each leg forward and backward gently, one at a time
- Bend your knees and squat down low, moving your upper body side-to-side
- Then gently lunge forward; one leg, then the other

Freestyle/Improvisation (5 minutes)
- Put on your favorite track and move freely to the beat
- Incorporate some basic moves, like the Two-Step, body rolls, or shoulder shimmies. Dance how you feel in the moment. Forget about how you look or if you're doing it "right"

Object Highlights in the Exhibition Section

The Godfather of Baltimore
August 1982
Reproduction
Photograph by Nicholas Kuskin

Altar Bust of Crystal LaBeija, Founding Mother of House of LaBeija
Julian Prairie, 2024
Clay and plaster
Courtesy of The Royal House of LaBeija

Mr. Wiggles Sessions Vol. #1 "King Tut Style"
Steffan Clemente
1990s
Private collection

View-Master Reels, "How to Breakdance" and "Meet the New York City Breakers"
1984
Jerome Robbins Dance Division, The New York Public Library for the Performing Arts, Astor, Lenox and Tilden Foundations

"Rock Steady vs. Dynamic Rockers"
Sedgwick and Ceder Vintage Clothing Co.
1982
Jerome Robbins Dance Division, The New York Public Library for the Performing Arts, Astor, Lenox and Tilden Foundations

Big Daddy Kane's Jacket and Pants
Dapper Dan
1992
Purple coated leather with chevron design
Collection of the Smithsonian National Museum of African American History and Culture, Gift of Big Daddy Kane

Paradise Garage Membership Card
1986 – 1987
Courtesy of Michele Saunders

Studio 54 Guest List
1978
Gift of Stephen Desroches, 2015

ARE WE ALL CITY YET? TRADITIONS REMIXED

New York City is a complicated yet vibrant melting pot, blending social dance traditions from across the globe. Beyond the countless block parties, community gatherings, religious festivities, and family events where these traditions are passed down, the city's dance floors are buzzing with new remixes, reimagining and building on the cultural legacies that inspired them. The 'remix' might occur aesthetically or through the practice of these social dances in spaces where they're not typically performed.

People practice these traditions throughout New York City, where the boundaries between music and dance genres are fluid, constantly shifting with new ideas. People often form lines and circles with two individuals or in groups, creating layers where people both lead and follow. They also add ways to be seen and appreciated in the dance form itself. In these spaces, traditions and shared futures are unapologetically celebrated.

Bhangra

Bhangra, originally from the Punjab region in India and Pakistan, has taken on a new life in New York City, where it's been infused with hip-hop, techno, and house beats by local DJs. The city's vibrant mix of cultures has brought energy to the dance with dancers blending traditional Bhangra with everything from Breaking to Rooted Jazz dances to the ever-popular Bollywood steps. This fusion reflects the diversity of the South Asian diaspora in New York City.

Dabka

Dabka, which translates to "stomping of feet" in Arabic, is a lively, energetic dance that's full of unity and history. Often performed at weddings, festivals, and reunions, it symbolizes the strength and continuity of cultural traditions.

In New York City, groups like Remix ⟷ Culture are reimagining these traditions by creating spaces where music, dance, video art, and storytelling come together. These events bring together traditional and contemporary influences, celebrating the rich cultures of Southwest Asia, North Africa, and the diaspora in NYC and around the world. In New York City, the Palestinian and Lebanese styles of the Dabka are the most common.

Yallah Habibi

Contra

The English-inspired dances of the 19th century are still going strong in New York City today. Whether it's Country Dance, New England Contra, or Square Dancing, these lively communities are reworking traditions with a modern spin.

Dance groups continue to thrive by blending the old with the new—reimagining music, dance choreographies, and who leads or follows in the dance. As these traditions evolve, space for intergenerational connections are created, with dancers of all ages coming together to celebrate their shared histories while pushing the boundaries of dance forms.

Are you a Left or Right?

Yiddish Dance

Following the devastation of Eastern European Jewish dance traditions during the Holocaust, Jewish survivors and communities in New York City have set out to preserve and reinvent Yiddish dances, using them as powerful symbols of survival and resilience. They began by blending traditional Yiddish dances with those tied to social activist movements, such as the Workers Circle Sher, to create a space for healing and multi-ethnic solidarity. By the 1970s, this cultural revival sparked a fresh, vibrant mix of Yiddish dance and music. More recently, the underground scene has embraced "Kleztronic" music—a fusion of electronic beats with traditional Klezmer—bringing a purposefully inclusive, modern spin to these historic dance forms.

Cumbia and Cumbia Sonidera

Cumbia, which hails from Colombia, has found new life in New York City, where it's constantly evolving through dance parties and live performances. These often transform parks and community gardens into vibrant spaces for people of all ages to connect.

A different style, known as Cumbia Sonidera, which originated in Mexico, adds electronic beats and the energy of sound system culture. It's a staple at underground clubs, massive discotheques, and street parties, where dancers synchronize to the ever-changing rhythms and the voices of sonideros—part DJ, part storyteller—who add their own flavor through using commentary between the songs.

Chinatown Block Party Bounce

A mashup of beloved records from different communities ignites the dance floors of Chinatown—and not just indoors. Block parties hosted by Think!Chinatown and Chinatown Records help bring music, passed down through generations, onto the streets. Community archivist and DJ, YiuYiu 瑶瑶, invites guest DJs to co-pilot with a mashup of songs that have brought dance floors to life across the East, Southeast, and South Asian diasporas. DJs play records ranging from Chinese Mambo and NYC Bhangra remixes to Cantonese pop music

Life is Now

Through Dance, We Remember. Through Dance, We Dream.

Native American Dances and the Powwow

New York City has one of the largest urban Native American/Indigenous populations in the country, representing a tremendous variety of peoples. Native people hold regular Powwows to celebrate living traditions and reconnect with far-flung families. These gatherings help to redefine "traditional" dance by incorporating or blending varied dance/music cultures of the Native peoples of the Americas and beyond. The music and dance are focal points of community building and serve as expressions of multi-tribe/nation unity, cultural continuity, and pride.

Dance & Movement Practice
Start Somewhere - Let's Try Bhangra

Suggested Song: "Daru Badnaam"
Artists: Kamal Kahlon & Param Singh

1. Bhangra Basic Step (Paranda Step)

- Stand with your feet about a hip's width apart
- Step one foot forward, tapping your heel to the ground (as if stepping over a puddle)
- Bring the foot back to center
- Repeat with the other foot
- Add arm movements: bend your arms at 90 degrees and lift them slightly as you step forward, then lower them as you step back

2. Sidestep (Jhumar Step)

- Start with your feet together
- Step to the side with your right foot (like you're taking a big step out)
- Bring the other foot to meet it
- Repeat, but start with your left foot
- Swing your arms gently in a circle as you step, keeping the movement light and flowing

3. Turn Step (Chakkar Step)

- Start with your feet together and bend your knees slightly
- Take a small step with your right foot, turning your body to the right as you do so
- Pivot on your left foot and turn 90 degrees, using your arms to guide the turn
- Repeat the turn with the opposite foot (left foot leading)

Call to Action
See You Outside

Most of the calls to action in this book encourage you to try social dance forms that may be new to you.

This call to action takes it a step further.

Many of the social dances in this chapter thrive in neighborhoods that strongly support the broader cultures from which these dances originate. Try them in a studio, but don't stop there—seek out where people are practicing in the streets, plazas, festivals, or gatherings at cultural centers. In some of these spaces, you might feel out of place. Be open to learning. Be humble. Check out options in the *Places to Learn, Practice, or Social Dance* section of this book. In New York City, the Dance Calendar is another good place to continue the journey.

Object Highlights in the Exhibition Section

Turntable (Technics), 1992
Mixer (RANE), 2010
Courtesy of DJ Rekha, Basement Bhangra

Dhol
Amb tree, mango wood, synthetic, and goat skin head
Courtesy of Sunny Jain, Founder/Bandleader of Red Baraat, 2002

Chuana Hembra and Chuana Macho
Henry de Jesus Ortiz Zabala
Selenicereus wood, beeswax, charcoal, and syringe cap
Courtesy of Melody Feo

Llamador, Tamboura, Tambor Alegre (Drums)
Marco Martínez, Tambores San Martín Tubara
Leather, rope, and wood
Private Collection: Karla Flórez School of Dance NY

Jewish Paper Cutting Installation
Jerise Fogel
2024
Strathmore drawing paper and watercolor paper
Scan this QR code for detailed information about the installation's writing, design, character, and place representations.

Collage of Records
Reproductions
Courtesy of Chinatown Records 華埠錄音

With Flying Colors
Annika Cheng
ca. 2024
Recycle textiles
Courtesy of Think!Chinatown

Freedom Dabka Performing at Brooklyn FAM: Festival of Arts and Music
Gregory Horan
2023
Courtesy of Gregory Horan

Thunderbird American Indian Dancers Performance
Jeenah Moon for *The New York Times*
2019
Reproduction
Courtesy of *The New York Times*/Redux

Conclusion

Urban Stomp is a way to curate spaces for learning through the body's senses, bringing together over 300 objects from major institutions and private lenders, many of which have never been publicly displayed before. This could only have been achieved through collaboration with various communities. The goal here is to expand on what one would normally see in a museum—broadening the scope.

"Urban" represents New York City's pulse, a place where cultures, ideas, and people find ways to be together. "Stomp" is that heartbeat—the rhythms that tie music and social dances together. It's the swingouts in Lindy Hop, the dips in Vogue, and the literal stomps in Dabka. These stomps connect different dance styles and cultures, creating a type of unity where each one tells a story of ancestry and dreams of a better tomorrow.

Return to this book when you create your own programs, parties, dance socials, or exhibits. *Urban Stomp* is not only a method but a call to action. The actions help manifest spaces where everyone has the opportunity to feel safe, knowing they are valued and that they matter.

As you reflect on your notes and ideas in this book, share them with the people you've met and put them into action. If you have the opportunity, return to the exhibit at the Museum of the City of New York and explore the 20+ electronic dance tutorials, the 11 immersive dance improvisation films in the exhibit's *Dancing Allowed!* section, 30+ archival dance films, dance regalia, and the ongoing public programs that happen at the museum and around New York City. Follow the author as *Urban Stomp* continues to expand, and its theory deepens. Let this book serve as a guide to inspire you, and may the dance floor always be an avenue for human connection, community, dreaming, and defiance against that which might rob us of our humanity.

Finding Defiant Joy Underneath, the Bridge

Urban Stomp Dance Tutorials Checklist

Check off the box once you've tried or viewed the exhibition dance tutorial.

Tutorial 1: Ragtime Dances

- ☐ The Castle Walk
- ☐ The Foxtrot

Tutorial 2: Rooted Solo Jazz Dances

- ☐ The Fall Off the Log
- ☐ The Boogie Forward/Boogie Backs/Fishtail

Tutorial 3: Solo and Partnered Rooted Jazz Dancing

- ☐ The Lindy Hop
- ☐ The Charleston

Tutorial 4: Salsa Dance Styles

- ☐ Salsa On2 (New York Salsa)
- ☐ Salsa Caleña (Colombian Salsa)
- ☐ Casino (Cuban Salsa)
- ☐ Salsa On3 and Dancing Salsa in the Home

Tutorial 5: Bachata Beats and Merengue Moves

- ☐ Bachata
- ☐ Merengue

Tutorial 6: Breaking Barriers

- ☐ Hustle
- ☐ Vogue

Tutorial 7: The Cypher

- ☐ Breaking
- ☐ Hip-hop Party Dances
- ☐ Litefeet

Tutorial 8: Traditions Remixed

- ☐ Dabka
- ☐ Contra
- ☐ Yiddish Dance
- ☐ Bhangra
- ☐ Cumbia Sonidera
- ☐ Cumbia

All Dancing Allowed! Checklist

Check the box once you've played the record AND danced in the exhibition's immersive dance floor experience, titled All Dancing Allowed!

- ☐ Bhangra
- ☐ Bachata
- ☐ Castle Walk
- ☐ Cumbia Sonidera
- ☐ Cumbia Colombiana
- ☐ Hip-hop
- ☐ House
- ☐ Hustle
- ☐ Lindy Hop
- ☐ Salsa
- ☐ Vogue

Exhibition Scavenger Hunt

Explore the exhibition by following the prompts in each section. As you move through the galleries, observe the dance steps, cultural influences, and objects that tell the story of dance throughout history. Reflect on how these movements have shaped and continue to evolve in today's world.

Use the space to take notes, track your discoveries, and uncover new insights. Each find is a chance to deepen your knowledge about the relationships between music and social dance cultures.

YOU ARE INVITED: BALLS, BALLROOMS & BARS

Which item is an accessory to the dress and gloves and helps keep you cool after dancing?

_____

What dance style contest was held at the Royal Mirror Hall in 1924?

_____

Who were the husband-and-wife duo who helped popularize Ragtime dance styles?

_____

IT DON'T MEAN A THING (IF IT AIN'T GOT THAT SWING)

Write down the names of at least three musicians and their instruments from the bandstand.

_____
_____

Who was known as the "King of Swing"?

_____

Which iconic dance group was Frankie Manning and Norma Miller members of?

_____

¡WEPA! FREEDOM DREAMS FROM MAMBO TO MERENGUE

Who is the owner of the Fania All-Stars jacket and wrote most of the songs on the iconic salsa album *Siembra*?

_____

Which dancer and musician are positioned next to each other in this section?

_____

Who was the featured singer in the song "Obsesión," by Aventura?

_____

THE CYPHER: BREAKS & BREAKING BARRIERS

Where did the famous battle between Rocksteady Crew and Dynamic Rockers take place on August 15, 1981?

Who owned the Dapper Dan suit featured in this section?

Which person started the house movement for LGTBQ+ people in NYC?

ARE WE ALL CITY YET? TRADITIONS REMIXED

Which DJ started the Basement Bhangra movement?

What's the name of the dance school that loaned the cumbia drums for the exhibition?

What does the word "Dabka" mean in Arabic?

ANSWER KEY

You Are Invited: Balls, Ballrooms & Bars
1. Fan
2. Waltz
3. Vernon and Irene Castle

It Don't Mean a Thing (If It Ain't Got That Swing)
1. Lester Young's New Wonder 1 tenor saxophone
   Cootie Williams's long-model cornet
   Miles Davis's trumpet
   Benny Goodman's clarinet
   Jack Teagarden's trombone
   Louis Armstrong's trumpet
2. Benny Goodman
3. Whitey's Lindy Hoppers

¡Wepa! Freedom Dreams from Mambo to Merengue
1. Rubén Blades
2. Eddie Torres and Tito Puente
3. Judy Santos

The Cypher: Breaks & Breaking Barriers
1. Lincoln Center for the Performing Arts
2. Big Daddy Kane
3. Crystal LaBeija

Are We All City Yet? Traditions Remixed
1. DJ Rekha
2. Karla Flórez School of Dance
3. "To stomp" or "stomping of the feet"

Places to Learn, Practice & Social Dance

- **Ballroom**
    - Vintage Dance Society
      https://vintagedance2.wixsite.com/vintagedancesociety
    - Danznik Studios
      https://www.danznik.com/studios/nyc/?utm_source=gmb&utm_medium=organic&utm_campaign=nyc
    - Big Apple Ballroom
      https://www.instagram.com/bigappleballroom

- **Lindy Hop**
    - Big Apple Lindy Hoppers
      https://www.instagram.com/bigapplelindyhoppers
    - Prohibition Productions
      https://www.prohibitionproductions.com/events

- **Salsa**
    - Salsa On2
        - Eddie and Maria Torres
          https://www.eddietorresny.com
        - Karel Flores
          https://www.instagram.com/karelflores/?hl=en
        - Piel Canela Dance School
          https://pielcaneladancers.com
        - Frankie Martinez Dance School
          https://www.frankiemartinez.org/nyc-classes
        - Latin Mondays at Taj hosted by Talia Castro-Pozo and classes with Marlon International
    - Salsa Caleña
        - Cali Salsa Pal Mundo
          https://www.instagram.com/calisalsanyc/?hl=en

- Cuban Salsa
  - Fuakata -Cuban Salsa NY
    https://www.instagram.com/fuakata_salsa_nyc/?hl=en
- Salsa Dance in the Home / Salsa On3
  - La Sala de Pepe
    https://www.lasaladepepe.org
  - Mama Juanas (Bronx), Salsa Tuesdays
    https://www.instagram.com/mamajuanabronx/?hl=en
- 116th Street Festival
  https://116thstfestival.com
- Orchard Beach Salsa Sundays
  Usually from noon until 5pm or 6pm, Plaza-Bandshell in Section 9
- 111th Street Old-Timers Day
  http://www.streetplay.com/events/111street2000.htm

- **Cumbia Sonidera Dance Classes and Music**
  - Mark Saldana
    https://www.instagram.com/coolmarx
  - Organization: Cumbia Classes
    https://www.instagram.com/cumbiadanceclasses/?hl=en
  - DJ: HelloTones (El Hijo de Puebla York)
    https://www.instagram.com/hellotones

- **Cumbia Colombiana**
  - Karla Flórez School of Dance
    https://www.instagram.com/karlaflorezsd/?hl=en
  - Rueda de Oro
    https://www.instagram.com/rueda_de_oro

- **Bhangra**
  - Basement Bhangra
    https://www.instagram.com/basementbhangra/?hl=en
  - Ajna Dance
    https://ajnadance.com
  - Bollywood Funk
    https://bollywoodfunknyc.com

- **Contra**
  - Brooklyn Contra
    https://www.brooklyncontra.org
  - Country Dance New York
    https://cdny.org

- **Dabka**
  - Freedom Dabka
    https://www.freedomdabka.com

- **Yiddish Dance**
  - Sarah Myerson
    https://cantorsarahmyerson.wixsite.com/cantor
  - Steve Weintraub
    https://www.stevenleeweintraub.com
  - Yiddish New York

- **Hustle**
  - NY Hustle Congress
    https://www.nyHustlecongress.com
  - New Style Hustle
    https://newstyleHustleworld.squarespace.com

- **Vogue**
  - Royal House of LaBeija
    https://www.royalhouseoflabeija.com
  - V House of New York
    https://www.instagram.com/vhouseofnewyork

- **Hip-hop**
  - Dynamic Rockers
    https://www.instagram.com/dynamicrockers/?hl=en
  - Lady Slic
    https://www.instagram.com/lady_slic
  - Kelly Peters, BrickHouse NYC
    https://www.instagram.com/kellypetersnyc/?hl=en
  - Every Body Move
    https://www.camilleabrown.org/everybodymove

Object Highlights in the Exhibition by Section

Chapter 1: You Are Invited: Balls, Ballrooms & Bars

Invitation, Ticket, and Dance Card for the Prince of Wales Ball
October 12, 1860
MCNY, Gift of Mrs. Stowe Phelps, 1961

"Order of Dancing at the Wedding of Mrs. Wells"
1865
Wood, white silk satin, white silk fringe, and gilt metallic trim
MCNY, Bequest of Miss Caroline Thorn Wells, 1950

Ball Gown
House of Worth, design house, designed by Charles Frederick Worth
1860
Silver and silk compound weave with peach ciselé velvet in floral and foliate motifs, white silk satin, and white silk lace
MCNY, Gift of Miss Sarah Gardiner, 1939

Fan
1850–60
Paper, mother-of-pearl, ink, paint, and silver-tone metal
MCNY, Bequest of Miss Katherine Van Wyck Haddock, 1951 (51.117.100)

Dance Shoes Worn by Irene Castle
Martin & Martin
ca. 1914
Orange and black silk satin and leather
MCNY, Gift of Mrs. Irene Castle, 1947

Hair Belonging to Irene Castle
Irene Castle
1914
Human hair
MCNY, Gift of Mrs. George Enzinger, 1948

Cylinder Phonograph
Edison Home Model A
The Edison Speaking Phonograph Company
1903
Metal and wood
MCNY, Gift of Rebecca, Amiel, and Juliet Weisfogel, 2025

Chapter 2: It Don't Mean a Thing (If It Ain't Got That Swing)

Josephine Baker Dancing the Charleston
Stanislaw Julian Ignacy Ostroróg, known as Walery
1926
Reproduction
National Portrait Gallery, Smithsonian Institution

Louis Armstrong's Trumpet
Selmer
1933
Steel and brass

Pages from Louis Armstrong's Manuscript Autobiography
1925
Courtesy of Institute of Jazz Studies, Rutgers University-Newark, Institute of Jazz Studies artifact collection

Untitled (Duke Ellington with Floating Piano)
Ed Dwight
ca. 1980
Bronze
Art & Artifacts Division, Schomburg Center for Research in Black Culture, The New York Public Library, Astor, Lenox and Tilden Foundations

The Frankie Manning Quilt
Jen Pringle
2009, tee-shirts from 1985 – 2009
Cotton quilt made of commemorative tee-shirts
Collection of Lana Turner, New York

Handbill, Savoy Ballroom
March 21, 1937
Courtesy of the International Lindy Hop Championships Museum

Benny Goodman's Clarinet
Buffet-Crampon
ca. 1960
Grenadilla, nickel-silver, plastic, and other materials
Lent by The Metropolitan Museum of Art, Gift of William F. Hyland, in memory of Theodore and Margaret Hyland, his parents, 1998

Lester Young's New Wonder 1 Tenor Saxophone
C. G. Conn
1914
Gold-plated brass
Courtesy of Institute of Jazz Studies, Rutgers University-Newark, Institute of Jazz Studies artifact collection

Cootie Williams's Long-Model Cornet
C. G. Conn
1968
Brass
Courtesy of Institute of Jazz Studies, Rutgers University-Newark, Institute of Jazz Studies artifact collection

Miles Davis's Trumpet
Martin
1964
Brass
Courtesy of Institute of Jazz Studies, Rutgers University-Newark, Institute of Jazz Studies artifact collection

Jack Teagarden's Trombone
C.G. Conn, mouthpiece made by Vincent Bach Corp.
ca. 1925
Brass, copper, and zinc alloy
Courtesy of Institute of Jazz Studies, Rutgers University-Newark, Institute of Jazz Studies artifact collection

Bracelets Worn by Billie Holiday
Metal and rhinestones
20th century
Courtesy of Institute of Jazz Studies, Rutgers University-Newark, Institute of Jazz Studies artifact collection

Chapter 3: ¡Wepa! Freedom Dreams from Mambo to Merengue

Dress owned by Celia Cruz
20th century
Quilted polyester
Courtesy of Celia Cruz Legacy Project

Shoes Owned by Celia Cruz
Miguel Nieto
20th century
Leather, rhinestones, satin, aluminum, vinyl, and rubber
Courtesy of Celia Cruz Legacy Project

Red Shirt, Pants, and Shoes Worn by Eddie Torres
Shoes by Alvarez Dance Shoes, shirt by Maria Torres, and pants by unknown maker
ca. 2017 – 2022
Shoes: leather; shirt: silk; and pants: polyester
Courtesy of Eddie Torres, Mambo King

Tito Puente's Timbales
Latin Percussion, Inc.
20th century
Steel, plastic, and ink with chrome plating
Courtesy of Tito Puente Jr.

Fania All-Stars Jacket Owned by Rubén Blades
ca. 1977
Wool and leather
Courtesy of Rubén Blades

Poster, "1er Festival del Merengue!"
1977
CUNY
Dominican Studies Institute Special Collections

Güira and Gancho
Blanco Custom
2019
Metal and wood
Courtesy of Areíto Arts

Aventura at an Awards Ceremony
2000s
Inkjet print
Courtesy of Juan and Judy Santos

Chapter 4: The Cypher: Breaks & Breaking Barriers

The Godfather of Baltimore
August 1982
Reproductions
Photograph by Nicholas Kuskin

Altar Bust of Crystal LaBeija, Founding Mother of House of LaBeija
Julian Prairie, 2024
Clay and plaster
Courtesy of The Royal House of LaBeija

Mr. Wiggles Sessions Vol. #1 "King Tut Style"
Steffan Clemente
1990s
Private collection

View-Master Reels, "How to Breakdance" and "Meet the New York City Breakers"
1984
Jerome Robbins Dance Division, The New York Public Library for the Performing Arts, Astor, Lenox and Tilden Foundations

"Rock Steady vs. Dynamic Rockers"
Sedgwick and Ceder Vintage Clothing C^{o}.
1982
Jerome Robbins Dance Division, The New York Public Library for the Performing Arts, Astor, Lenox and Tilden Foundations

Big Daddy Kane's Jacket and Pants
Dapper Dan
1992
Purple coated leather with chevron design
Collection of the Smithsonian National Museum of African American History and Culture, Gift of Big Daddy Kane

Paradise Garage Membership Card
1986 – 1987
Courtesy of Michele Saunders

Studio 54 Guest List
1978
Gift of Stephen Desroches, 2015

Chapter 5: Are We All City Yet? Traditions Remixed

Turntable (Technics), 1992
Mixer (RANE), 2010
Courtesy of DJ Rekha, Basement Bhangra

Dhol
Amb tree, mango wood, synthetic, and goat skin head
Courtesy of Sunny Jain, Founder/Bandleader of Red Baraat, 2002

Chuana Hembra and Chuana Macho
Henry de Jesus Ortiz Zabala
Selenicereus wood, beeswax, charcoal, and syringe cap
Courtesy of Melody Feo

Llamador, Tamboura, Tambor Alegre (Drums)
Marco Martínez, Tambores San Martín Tubara
Leather, rope, and wood
Private Collection: Karla Flórez School of Dance NY

Jewish Paper Cutting Installation
Jerise Fogel
2024
Strathmore drawing paper and watercolor paper
Scan this QR code for detailed information about the installation's writing, design, character, and place representations.

Collage of Records
Reproductions
Courtesy of Chinatown Records 華埠錄音

With Flying Colors
Annika Cheng
ca. 2024
Recycled textiles
Courtesy of Think!Chinatown

Freedom Dabka Performing at Brooklyn FAM: Festival of Arts and Music
Gregory Horan
2023
Courtesy of Gregory Horan

Thunderbird American Indian Dancers Performance
Jeenah Moon for *The New York Times*
2019
Reproduction
Courtesy of *The New York Times/Redux*

About the Author

Dr. Derrick León Washington is a cultural anthropologist, dancer, and curator. Working in partnership with Sarah Henry, he is the curator of *Urban Stomp: Dreams & Defiance on the Dance Floor.*

With over ten years of curatorial experience, his contributions to the *Urban Stomp* exhibition include object acquisition, artistic installation research, ethnographic research, cultivating relationships with communities, artists, and lending institutions, writing object labels, producing dance tutorial films, as well as overseeing the overall development of the exhibition. His curatorial work has garnered positive reviews from major media outlets, such as *The New York Times*, the BBC, ARTE (Europe), *New York Post*, UN Web TV, El Especialito, *The Huffington Post*, *Le Monde* (France), UN Department of Global Communications, UN News, and NBC.

At United Nations Headquarters in New York City, Dr. Washington curated several projects for the UN Human Rights division. These included a multi-national arts/human rights webinar series, the development and moderation of the final plenary at the United Nations Economic and Social Council (ECOSOC) 10th Anniversary Youth Forum 2021, United Nations International Day of the World's Indigenous Peoples (2021), the first United Nations International Day for People of African Descent (2021), the ongoing multi-agency United Nations Art Collection project, UNHQ Visitor Services webisodes, and several UN films, including a short film about the 'I Still Believe in Our City' campaign, sponsored by UN Human Rights (OHCHR) and the NYC Commission on Human Rights.

He is also the curator of *Rhythm & Power: Salsa in New York* (2017), a groundbreaking exhibition and expansive, interactive program series on Salsa as an artistic social movement presented at the Museum of the City of New York. The exhibition's program series is the most expansive program series in terms of programmatic diversity ever created. Building upon his curatorial work, Dr. Washington is the co-editor of the book, *Rhythm & Power: Performing Salsa in Puerto Rican and Latino Communities* (Centro Publications, 2017). Dr. Washington was also featured as an expert speaker and worked as a consultant for the documentary, *Nueva York: A Musical History of Latin New York* (2021). Featured on the ARTE television network, the documentary was broadcasted in over 22 European countries. It received a positive review in one of France's most influential and widely circulated newspapers, *Le Monde*.

Dr. Washington is also the director and curator of *Urban Stomp: From Swing to Mambo*. The project features an interactive program series across NYC and a documentary short film, which laid the foundations for a lecture-performance at Lincoln Center for the Performing Arts in 2019. In 2022, the project expanded with a documentary collaboration with the Apollo Theater and a teaching artist training series at Rutgers University.

With the support of the Museum of the City of New York, he curated *Urban Stomp: Dreams & Defiance on the Dance Floor* (2025 – 2026). As the first museum exhibition to explore the social dances that influence not only the dance floor, but also the world beyond it, the exhibit showcases over 300 objects. These include ephemera, contemporary art installations, monuments, photographs, mid-1800's ball dance cards, ball gowns, ceremonial regalia, costumes, sculptures, film, musical instruments, a dance map, life-size electronic dance tutorials, and a gallery celebrating a city-wide mashup dance party, evoking the spirit of NYC's iconic dance spaces. Public and educational programs are offered both at the museum and across New York City. The exhibition is on extended display from April 2025 to February 2026.

As an active choreographer, dancer, and instructor, he assembled over 90 dancers and cultural practitioners to produce more than 20 dance tutorial videos and immersive dance floor experiences for the *Urban Stomp* exhibition.

As a cultural anthropologist, he conducted archival and participant observation research across a wide range of dance communities, from the Foxtrot to Bhangra, gaining a deeper understanding of the diverse dance cultures represented in the exhibition. He has an undergraduate degree in cultural anthropology from the University of California at Los Angeles. He completed his master's degree, curatorial portfolio certificate, and doctorate in socio-cultural anthropology at the University of Texas at Austin.

For further information:

Scan the QR code or visit, *www.urbanstomp.org*

https://www.facebook.com/derricklwashington1

@derricklwashington1

Exhibition: *https://www.mcny.org/exhibition/urban-stomp*

About the Illustrator

Originally from Dnipro, Ukraine, **Olha Aleksandrova** has been passionate about art and making art since she was a child. Graduating from art school, she later studied academic drawing while pursuing a degree in architecture. In Ukraine, Olha worked as a lead architect while also teaching fashion illustration and painting.

In addition to taking on commissions, Olha shares her creative journey through a blog and continues to grow as an artist, constantly exploring new ways to express her vision through art.

For Olha, drawing is as natural and essential as breathing—it's both a passion and a commitment that shapes her life and defines who she is.

https://aleksroom.com

@olechka__boss

Exhibition Dance Video Tutorial Film Credits

Produced by Derrick León Washington
Filmed by Earthbound Studios

You Are Invited: Balls, Ballrooms & Bars

    Castle Walk / Foxtrot: Marc Casslar & Martha Griffin – *Vintage Dance Society*

It Don't Mean a Thing (If It Ain't Got That Swing)

    Lindy Hop: Nathan Bugh & Elena Valencia

    Solo Jazz: Candice Franklin-Cox (Charleston), Jaime Shannon (Tacky Annie) & Elena Valencia (Boogie Back / Boogie Forward / Fishtail)

¡Wepa! Freedom Dreams from Mambo to Merengue

    Salsa On2: Karel Flores & Bruno Rodriguez

    Cuban Salsa: Christopher Rogicki & Nilka Acosta, *Fuákata – Cuban Salsa NY*

    Colombian Salsa: Jhonathan "Kiko" Ramos & Vivien Reyes – *Cali Salsa Pal Mundo*

    Salsa On3 / Salsa in the Home: José "Pepe" Flores & Maria Noel Costa – *La Sala de Pepe*

    Bachata: Angely Francisco & Beverly Lopez – *¡Dame Tu Pasito!*

    Merengue: Joe Burgos & Bianca Soto – *Piel Canela Dance Company*

The Cypher: Breaks & Breaking Barriers

    Vogue: LeFierce LaBeija – *The Royal House of LaBeija*

    Hustle: Lori Brizzi & Ron Rosario

    Breaking: Victor "Kid Glyde" Alicea – *Dynamic Rockers*

Hip-Hop Party Dances: Ethel Calhoun, Malaika Holder & Maxine Montilus –*Camille A. Brown & Dancers / Every Body Move*

Litefeet: Chiquita "Lady Slic" Harrell & Mo the Dancer

Are We All City Yet? Traditions Remixed

Cumbia Colombiana: Karla Flórez, Enrique Olaya & Valentina Olaya-Flórez –*Karla Flórez School of Dance*

Bhangra: Minila Shah – *Ajna Dance*

Dabka: Amer Abdelrasoul, Sharon Chin, Martha Edwards & Derrick León Washington – *Freedom Dabka Group* (Amer Abdelrasoul)

Yiddish Dance: Sarah Myerson, Ilja Sneiveiss, Sarah Chandler, Sharon Chin, Martha Edwards, Chelsea Simon, Beila Ungar, Derrick León Washington & Rachel Wetter

Cumbia Sonidera: Mark Saldana & Gerardo Veliz

Contra: Alyssa Adkins, Sarah Henry, Evan Kohne, Christin Licata, Stephan Luma, Andrea Murray, John Rinehart

Exhibition Immersive Dance Floor Film Credits

Produced by Derrick León Washington
Filmed by Earthbound Studios

Salsa
Karel Flores & Friends
Featuring Karel Flores with Juan Carlos Diaz, Edwin Tolentino, Antoy Juliana WonPat-Borja, and dancers from Harlem School of the Arts
Music: "Timbalaye" by Los Hacheros

Bachata
Redi Dance Company
Featuring REDi Dance Company with Beverly Lopez, Kirée Brooks, Tyree Rainey, and Chris Donald
Music: "Como Te Lo Mereces" by Savi Rodriguez

Lindy Hop
Big Apple Lindy Hoppers
Featuring Big Apple Lindy Hoppers with Skyler Barr, Samuel Coleman, Bernadette Cumento, Sam Hindle, Tawni M. Lanford, Stanislas Lauly, Devon Lawler, Ruoyi Ma, Adrian Miranda, Thomas J. Savino, Johnny Schlender, Tank Tan, Jason Zheng, and dancers from Harlem School of the Arts
Music: "You Made Me Love You" by The Hot Toddies Jazz Band

Castle Walk
Vintage Dance Society
Featuring Vintage Dance Society with Kandie Carle, Marc Casslar, Martha Griffin, Michele Massa, Jean McCabe, and Joe Missbrenner
Music: "Too Much Mustard by One Step" by Layman H. Jones.

House
Gen X
Featuring Gen X at Brickhouse NYC with McKinley Alston, Tyler Buzzell, Rashaan Evans, Una Lin, Lisbeth Tavarez, and dancers from Harlem School of the Arts
Music: "Mixing Room" by DJ Qu

Hip Hop
Gen X
Featuring Gen X at Brickhouse NYC with McKinley Alston, Tyler Buzzell, Rashaan Evans, Una Lin, Lisbeth Tavarez, and dancers from Harlem School of the Arts

Vogue
The Royal House of LaBeija
Featuring Royal House of LaBeija with Angel LaBeija, Frida LaBeija, Jeffrey LaBeija, LeFierce LaBeija, and dancers from Harlem School of the Arts
Music: "I'm a Woman" by Kevin Jz Prodigy

Hustle
NY Hustle Congress
Featuring NY Hustle Congress with Lori Brizzi, Robert Finocchio, Gaga Newburn, Sal Rentas, and dancers from Harlem School of the Arts

Cumbia Sonidera
Mark Saldana & Friends
Featuring Mark Saldana with Edelin Garcia Quiroz, Eric Garcia Quiroz, Juan Mendez, Ashley Ogando, Luis Perez, Joel Tepi, Albino Gerardo Victorio Veliz, and dancers from Harlem School of the Arts
Music: "Mi Bella Cumbiamberita" by Joaquín Pérez

Bhangra
Bollywood Funk
Featuring Bollywood Funk with Rashmi Ketha, Sandhya Kilambi, Diksha Mishra, Jaya Sinha, and dancers from Harlem School of the Arts
Music: "Basement Bhangra Anthem" by DJ Rekha

Cumbia
Karla Flórez School of Dance
Featuring Karla Flórez School of Dance with Elvira Bustamante, Jennifer Cabana, Karla Flórez, Julián Gómez, Néstor Gómez, Angelika Jaramillo, José Lozano, Kike Olaya, Valentina Olaya-Flórez, and Carlos Rienzo

Bibliography

Abreu, Christina D. *Rhythms of Race: Cuban Musicians and the Making of Latino New York City and Miami, 1940–1960.* Chapel Hill: University of North Carolina Press, 2015.

Agurto Espinoza, Andrés. *Salsa Consciente: Politics, Poetics, and Latinidad in the Meta-Barrio.* Michigan State University Press, 2022.

Berríos-Miranda, Marisol. "Salsa Music as Expressive Liberation." *CENTRO: Journal of the Center for Puerto Rican Studies* 16, no. 2 (2004): 157–173.

Chasteen, John Charles. *National Rhythms, African Roots: The Deep History of Latin American Popular Dance.* New edition. Albuquerque: University of New Mexico Press, 2004.

DeFrantz, Thomas F., ed. *Dancing Many Drums: Excavations in African American Dance.* Madison: University of Wisconsin Press, 2002.

Denzin, Norman K. *Performance Ethnography: Critical Pedagogy and the Politics of Culture.* Thousand Oaks, CA: Sage Publications, 2003.

Flores, Juan. *From Bomba to Hip-Hop: Puerto Rican Culture and Latino Identity.* New York: Columbia University Press, 2000.

Flores, Juan. *Salsa Rising: New York Latin Music of the Sixties Generation.* New York: Oxford University Press, 2016.

Gottschild, Brenda Dixon. *Digging the Africanist Presence in American Performance: Dance and Other Contexts.* Westport: Praeger Publishers, 1996.

Guarino, Lindsay, Carlos R. A. Jones, and Wendy Oliver, eds. *Rooted Jazz Dance: Africanist Aesthetics and Equity in the Twenty-First Century.* University Press of Florida, 2022.

Hamera, Judith. *Dancing Communities: Performance, Difference, and Connection in the Global City.* Edited by Janelle Reinelt and Brian Singleton. New York:

Palgrave Macmillan, 2007.

McMains, Juliet E. *Spinning Mambo into Salsa: Caribbean Dance in Global Commerce.* New York: Oxford University Press, 2015.

Malnig, Julie, ed. *Ballroom, Boogie, Shimmy Sham, Shake: A Social and Popular Dance Reader.* Urbana: University of Illinois Press, 2009.

Washington, Derrick León, Priscilla Renta, and Sydney Hutchinson. *Rhythm & Power.* Centro Press, Center for Puerto Rican Studies, Hunter College of City University of New York, 2017.

www.ingramcontent.com/pod-product-compliance
Lightning Source LLC
Chambersburg PA
CBRC091208010526
44107CB00022B/1264